Gadgets for Singing

INVENTIVE AND INEXPENSIVE TOOLS TO EMPOWER YOUR SINGERS

By Christy Elsner

ISBN 978-1-4803-42686-6

Shawnee Press

EXCLUSIVELY DISTRIBUTED BY

HAL•LEONARD® CORPORATION

7777 W. BLUEMOUND RD. P.O. BOX 13819 MILWAUKEE, WI 53213

In Australia Contact:
Hal Leonard Australia Pty. Ltd.
4 Lentara Court
Cheltenham, Victoria, 3192 Australia
Email: ausadmin@halleonard.com.au

Visit Shawnee Press Online at
www.shawneepress.com

Visit Hal Leonard Online at
www.halleonard.com

Table of Contents

Foreword

As a music educator, are you stuck in a choral pedagogy rut? Research now suggests that students' brains are being "rewired" due to the technological gadgets they use; therefore, doesn't it make sense that the ways we teach choral music and pedagogy need to be "rewired" as well? Don't get me wrong...I am not suggesting choral educators become entertainers. However, we must "rewire" our teaching methods to capture the attention of singers, to help them connect to the emotional side of singing, and to retain the numbers in choral programs.

Personally, the use of "gadgets" in a choral setting is invaluable to me and my singers. With a gadget in hand, every singer is physically engaged in the learning process, as well as the discovery of their individual voice. Using a "gadget" to teach fundamentals provides endless kinesthetic opportunities as well as providing innovative and unique rehearsal experiences.

In this handy resource, you'll find 30 top "gadgets" that have helped my singers. Introduce a new gadget once a week and see what happens to your ensemble! Here are some ideas to implement that will refresh and invigorate your bag of teaching tools:

1. Get out from behind the piano! Step off the podium and "mix it up" with your singers.

2. Unleash your creative beast; be BOLD!

3. Referring to gadgets as Learning Tools will create the highest expectations that you have for the group as well as create an environment of trust between you and the singers.

4. The best recruitment tool you have is an inventive and energetic classroom.

5. Many vocal skills require daily reinforcement until they become a habit. When tempted to explain the "ah" vowel in the same way as yesterday, use a gadget! If you are bored with the presentation, it is likely that your students also feel the same way!

6. Using gadgets in your choral rehearsal doesn't have to be expensive. Try some of the following ideas:

    a. Support from PTO (Parent-Teacher Organization) or local organizations

    b. Grants

    c. Donations

    d. Contests

    e. Ordinary stuff (items in the garage, kitchen, basement, drawers, etc.)

Giving our singers "tools" or "gadgets" to increase self-awareness and engage both sides of the brain increases rehearsal productivity and efficiency while eliciting passion...which yields an unforgettable choral experience for you and your students!

Christy Elsner

CHAPTER 1

The Cookie

*A*ll singers, young or mature, need constant and consistent reminders of the ideal lip shape and mouth space. Using a cookie is a great tool for creating a uniform sound (especially "ah," "eh," and "oh") without a lengthy, monotonous speech from you about vowel or tone formation. By using a cookie in the ways listed below, the transformation of sound is amazingly quick and evident!

Introducing the Cookie Gadget

1. Hand out one cookie (or similar edible item) to each singer. Instruct the singers to place the cookie horizontally in the front of their mouths. With the cookie in this position, lead a warm-up, a single note, or a phrase; the mouth and lips imitate the shape of the cookie.

2. Next, tell the singers to turn their cookie vertically to create a tall, lifted space between their lips and teeth. Sing the same warm-up, single note, or a phrase of lyrics imitating the shape of the cookie.

3. Lead a discussion with the singers regarding the differences in sound and physical sensations between the horizontal and the vertical placement of the cookie.

Tips:

1. *When holding the cookie vertically, the student can bite into the top of the cookie with two top teeth, thus creating a lift instead of pulling the jaw downward.*

2. *Place the cookie between the cheekbone and the lower jawbone. Encourage the singers to remember how this feels and to keep this space open which will create resonance and an open throat.*

CHAPTER 2

Food and the Five Basic Vowels

Apple

An apple is a great gadget for teaching the "ah" vowel (ah-pple). Although the choral director can demonstrate the exercise with one apple, participation from the entire class is more effective. Encourage the singers to remember the sensation they feel when biting in the apple with top two teeth to create a lifted, forward "ah" vowel sound. Keep an apple handy in the choral room to hold up every now and then as a reminder.

Lemon

The lemon is a great gadget to illustrate the "eh" vowel as it tends to fall to the back of the throat for singers. One end of the lemon is pointed, thus representing the peak placement of the "eh" inside the roof of the mouth, right behind the front teeth. An egg has a similar shape to a lemon and can be used as well.

Cheese

Break out the sliced cheese and distribute a slice to each singer. Tell them to bite a hole in the cheese. The lips are represented by the square part of the cheese and the sound goes right through the hole "oo" of the cheese. Cheesy lips. 🙂

Orange

Use an orange to reinforce the "oh" vowel shape. Often singers close their lips to an "oo" or "uh" shape, resulting in a closed-off throat. Place the orange on the "cheek" to illustrate space.

Blueberries

Distribute a blueberry to each student and instruct them to put the small fruit between their lips and sing. Next, each kid will pull out their blueberry and keep singing the "oo," creating the correct physical sensation.

Potato chips in a cylinder container

Gretchen Harrison, a choral colleague, invented this exercise using the chips that can be bought in a cylinder container as they demonstrate the mechanics of mouth space and shape in relation to the lips and throat. Place the chip on top of the tongue and attempt to sing. Point out to the singers that keeping the tongue flat versus arching the tongue affects resonation, impacts the sounds coming from the vocal cords, and affects certain consonants.

CHAPTER 3

Kitchen Utensils

Kitchens are a great place to find cool and interesting gadgets to use in your vocal pedagogy instruction (and food is a focus tool for singers of any age).

Whisk

Whisk oil and water in a clear glass bowl. The results demonstrate the importance of blending. Oil and water are like two different vowel shapes for the same vowel; they just won't mix!

Knife

Plastic picnic knives can be used to teach singing with separation, staccato, and marcato, as well as with accents. How quick or heavy the knife chops a carrot can illustrate how sound can be articulated by singers. Use the knife for agility work such as melismas in Baroque music. It can also be used in combination with the next kitchen gadget, a spatula or frosting knife for phrasing.

Spatula/Frosting Knife

Creating beautiful, legato notes that meld into one another can prove to be a difficult task. A spatula can be used instead of a conducting baton to show the image of "spreading the sound." A frosting knife can demonstrate the same concept of creating a continuous smooth sound. Bring a whole new level of interest to your classroom and allow the students to spread frosting on a piece of cardstock or a paper plate while singing.

Measuring Cups

Most singers comfortably sing in a mezzo forte range. Encourage your singers to broaden their dynamic scale capabilities. Use measuring cups and spoons to illustrate a difference in dynamic levels. Singers can visually see the proportionate difference between 1/8 teaspoon of water and 1 cup of water. Pairing dynamic markings with the different levels opens them to dynamic level possibilities. Using measuring utensils is also effective when achieving a gradual decrescendo or crescendo.

Cake Pans

Like a cake, a piece of music can have multiple layers of sound and emotion using tempo, meter, modality, melody, harmony, dynamics, diction, etc. By building a "layered cake" for each song, singers can grasp the importance of each layer as well as what is involved to achieve a successful end result.

Tongs

Use kitchen tongs to demonstrate the following:
- Vertical vs. horizontal sound
- A flat tongue
- Crisp, precise consonants at the end of a phrase
- Release of a word or breath without closing the lips

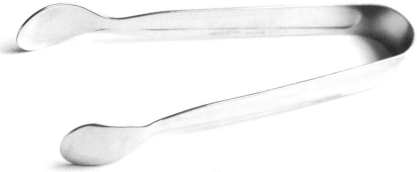

CHAPTER 4

The Marshmallow

$\mathcal{M}$arshmallows can be an effective gadget when the desired sound is full, open, and resonant, especially in music such as spirituals or German chorales. In fact, marshmallows may be your saving grace!

Marshmallows come in all sizes, including huge "campfire" marshmallows. Try different sizes to illustrate the different amounts of space needed.

1. Insert a large-sized marshmallow into the mouth with the flat side on the tongue.

2. Sing the phrase or the entire song without letting the roof of the mouth touch the top of the marshmallow.

By inserting a marshmallow in the mouth, the singer cannot close off the sound that is needed for the full tone of a spiritual or the tall, open, and warm sound of a Brahms' piece. OK...there may be some marshmallow juice escaping out of the corner of a mouth, but the overall sensation will be cemented in the singer's brain! Singers experience sound without closing for consonants.

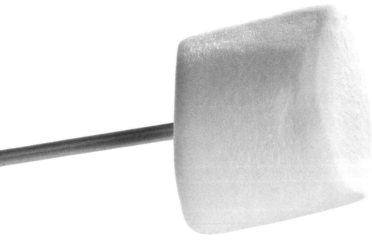

CHAPTER 5

Straws

*S*traws offer a unique and inexpensive opportunity for students to experience the sensation of breath.

The Big Gulp

Work with a local convenience store or gas station to acquire a donation of 32 oz. (or larger) cups and long straws. A huge beverage cup and long straw allow singers to feel a "full breath" sensation.

- Instruct the singers to place the straw in the empty cup.

- When cued, the singers should attempt to suck up the entire cup of air in 5-10 seconds. Singers should immediately experience the outward expansion of the lower belly and lower ribcage, front and back.

- Discuss the sensation or ask the students to journal the sensations they felt doing this exercise.

- Next, give out tiny disposable cups to experiment with the difference of the big cup versus the little cup.

- Decrease the amount of time to suck up the entire "big gulp" from ten seconds to only one second.

Cool Air

Singers can use the straw to feel cool air pass by the vocal folds, ensuring the breath is not coming from the shoulder area, but the engaged abdominals.

CHAPTER 6

Toothpicks

Once singers can visualize and manufacture correct vowel formation with the lips, sometimes the area in the back of the mouth and throat collapse and are forgotten. The toothpick is a helpful tool in the following ways:

- Hold a toothpick up to the side of the singer's face. Ask the student to sing while keeping their top and bottom molars away from the toothpick.

- A toothpick is effective at keeping the "eh" vowel from falling backward and sounding swallowed. Choose a favorite warm-up that includes an "eh" vowel. Place the toothpick at the jaw hinge or by the corner of the mouth. When singing the "eh" vowel, rotate the tip of the toothpick forward.

- When seeking a clean sound for running notes (as in Baroque melismas), use the tip of the toothpick to tap the beat on a folder or on the back of a hand. The weight of the toothpick emulates light "sound."

- Dip a toothpick into paint and tap the color emulating the clarity needed for running sixteenth notes in the music.

- Two toothpicks make perfect "goalposts" to place on the corners of the mouth while keeping the corners tucked in for all vowel shapes.

Tip:

Only choir members who have proven to be trustworthy can use the toothpick as a gadget. Students can rise to any occasion. When clear boundaries are set and maintained, a toothpick can be used, without injury, in the choral setting.

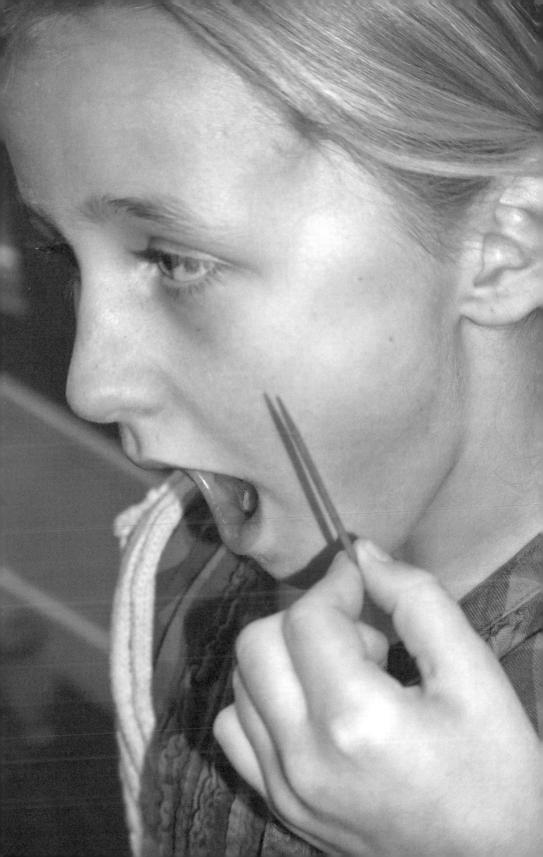

CHAPTER 7

Candy

*Y*oung singers will do about anything for a candy reward!

Chocolate

Place a piece of chocolate on the front of the tongue. Sing. The singers will find this is an effective way to encourage a flat, relaxed tongue when singing.

Place a piece of chocolate that has a "peak" further back on the tongue. Sing without letting the roof of the mouth touch the "peak." The use of this gadget promotes an open throat and lifted soft palate.

Bubble Gum

Oh, yeah – your custodial crew will "love" you...but bubble gum has multiple uses in the choir setting as a gadget.

The action of chewing bubble gum stretches and warms up the facial muscles, especially when given clear instructions on how to chew.

Bubbles can only be blown if the abdominal muscles and breathing mechanism are engaged. Don't believe me? Try blowing a bubble with breath from your shoulders – it just doesn't work!

You can "double the bubble fun" by holding a bubble-blowing contest with prizes for the biggest and best bubbles.

Peppermints or Breath Strips

Candy is a great motivator in almost any situation! By using round peppermint candy or breath strips, the breath process can be unique and memorable.

- Give each singer a piece of peppermint candy or a breath strip upon entering the rehearsal. The singers, if breathing correctly with open throats and abdominals, will feel "cool air" pass through their throats.

- The minty feeling should last at least 15-20 minutes into the rehearsal.

- Use the "cool air" feeling with breathing exercises during warm-ups.

- The peppermint candy can be used to reinforce the importance of space between the back molars for ultimate resonance and tone production. Mature and responsible singers should place the round peppermint between their back molars and sing. They will immediately feel a spatial difference.

Tip:

If time is of the essence, many brands of breath strips melt instantly on one's tongue!

CHAPTER 8

Bowls

*B*eginning swimmers spend several minutes during each lesson learning to blow bubbles in the water. In fact, my daughter was taught to hum a song while blowing bubbles in the water to keep the water from entering her nose! In order to blow bubbles in water, abdominals and the breathing mechanism must be engaged. The same concept to create swimmer's bubbles also applies to young singers. Blowing bubbles while singing releases tension from the tongue, relaxes the larynx, and helps increase stamina.

Below is an amusing and productive activity to use with this gadget for an outdoor activity on a beautiful spring or autumn day when the barometric pressure changes!

- Ask students to bring disposable plastic bowls or containers from home (butter tubs or whipped topping containers work great).

- Fill the bowls with enough water for singers to buzz their lips loosely or "motorboat" the water in the bowl.

- Blow bubbles in the water for a given period of time.

- Increase the periods of time to improve longevity of breath.

Bowls are also a great gadget for older singers who are experiencing a difficult spot in the music, a break in their tessitura, or need to sing through a phrase without a breath.

CHAPTER 9

Paintbrushes and Paint

Combining the "art" of song with the "art" of painting increases self-expression in your singers while supporting tactile learning. Just put a paintbrush in your singers' hands and step back to see the results. Visual learners will click instantly to musical expression qualities. The benefits with this gadget are endless!

- With a paintbrush in each hand, a choir can work on phrase contouring, articulation, dynamics, word stress, diction, and even vowel formation.

- Use paint, paper, and a paintbrush to illustrate the phrasing of a song as a group, as individuals, or entire choir project.

- Instruct singers or small groups to paint what they envision to be the meaning or story of a song.

- Paint a "road map" of the entire song, giving each student a few measures to paint. Combine each artist's work together to make a huge mural for the song.

- Using paint and paintbrushes creates a vital link to art elements and history with sound (i.e., text painting, Pointillism, Renaissance, Impressionism, etc.)

CHAPTER 10

Rubber Bands

Rubber bands are simple, inexpensive, and readily available gadgets that help teach breath, dynamics, an open throat, and a forward sound. Keep a rubber band on your wrist and call it a "Learning Tool" from Day 1. Use rubber bands in the following ways:

- A rubber band is a quick remedy when working to achieve a quiet, swift breath and a controlled release. Place the rubber band between the thumbs and index fingers of both hands.

- Place it near the belly button for emphasis on lower abdominal work.

- Rubber bands can aid a singer in his/her understanding of crescendos and diminuendos. Control the tension in the rubber band to illustrate the change in dynamic. The diminuendos will not collapse as singers connect the rubber band to breath.

- Singers need constant instruction and reminders of the concept of an open throat as well as keeping the sound forward. By placing the rubber band near the jaw area, singers mentally connect the open rubber band with the open jaw hinge. By placing the rubber band in the center of the forehead, it will pull the sound forward as the choir sings warm-ups or a passage from a song.

- A rubber band can be used for leaps or upper-register work. Hold a rubber band on the forehead and pull the rubber band, pulling the sound from the top of the head.

CHAPTER 11

Sponges

Sponges (slightly damp) can be a kinesthetic wonder. It is challenging for singers to vocally express emotions. As a choral educator, it is important to find new ways to teach control of the breath as well as techniques for singers to increase emotional connections with music. Give each singer a sponge to use as a choral gadget and introduce some of the below techniques:

- Is phrasing a problem? When working within a phrase, squeeze the sponge on important words.

- Do you have singers who unintentionally sneak in a breath in the middle of a phrase? Instruct the singers to squeeze their sponges immediately when sound is produced and to release the sponge when given a cut-off after singing a phrase. The act of keeping the sponge in "squeeze" mode serves as a reminder to not breathe during the phrase. This also helps singers to release the breath more gently and completely.

- Conversely, some singers struggle with a glottal approach to initial sound, stopping the air between the initial intake of breath and the start of sound production. The student can use this gadget to squeeze the sponge during the intake of air and to release the sponge when starting the sound production.

CHAPTER 12

Helical Spring / Coil

*S*ingers can take a successful breath to produce a perfect initial sound, but keeping the sound moving forward with energy in long passages can be a challenge for young singers. Try a helical spring that stretches and can bounce up and down (the most popularly-named is a Slinky® toy)!

- Your singers can use the coil during slow passages or difficult legato passages in their music. Place ends of the helical spring in each palm of the hand and move the coil back and forth during the long and/or legato phrases. This kinesthetic motion encourages singers to keep the air moving.

- The coil can also help with rubato in phrases. Encourage rubato singing with singers feeling the tempo as they move the coil faster or slower to match the music.

- The spring/coil can also aid the singers to feel the dynamics within a phrase by increasing or decreasing the space between the different hands as they move up or down, depending on the dynamics in the score.

Tip:

As a kid, I loved the traditional metal Slinky® toy. For use in the choral classroom, the plastic coil seems to withstand use and tangling better than the metal toy.

CHAPTER 13

Stickers

Stickers are economical constructive gadgets that offer endless opportunities for growth and musicianship. Thanks to early education teachers, stickers already have a positive image with students; who doesn't love getting sticker?

- Strategically place stickers on areas of resonance on the face, encouraging singers to feel the sensation where the stickers are placed. This is an excellent way to work within the resonating "mask" and lift the facial cheeks.

- A quick way to get the singers to engage their faces is to place stickers just above the eyebrows and ask singers to raise the stickers with every intake of breath.

- Affix stickers on kids' shoulder blades; you'll be amazed how the posture instantly improves without a director's soliloquy on posture!

- For singers who tend to clasp their hands together in front or back of the body, use stickers on the sides of jeans, pants, or skirts to give the singers a guide of where the hands should be placed when singing.

Tip:

Time is of the essence in rehearsal and it is difficult to acknowledge an individual's efforts in a group setting. Use different colored stickers to make a non-verbal statement about any skill that you wish to reinforce with the chorus. For example, a blue sticker on a singer's forehead represents perfect posture while a red sticker represents a choir member singing with expression.

CHAPTER 14

Masks

$\mathcal{I}$t can be a difficult concept for young singers (and experienced singers) to understand singing in the "mask." Why not use an actual mask to encourage resonant singing? Party and craft stores sell packages of multiple plastic masks. Distribute a mask to each singer.

Use the mask as a choral gadget with these activities:

- Singers can wear the mask during targeted warm-ups to encourage identification of placement of sound in the mask.

- Vocalists can wear a mask while singing a song to replicate the sensation that occurred during warm-ups.

- The students can wear the mask to feel the resonation sensation while singing a siren, a warm-up, or a song with teeth open and lips closed.

Tip:

If you are always looking for a non-singing activity to round out a retreat or provide an activity for a teacher, allow the singers to decorate their individual masks with glitter, beads, pearls, or paint pens.

CHAPTER 15

Descriptors

Engage the verbally talented choir members to lead a brainstorm session and create a list of descriptors (i.e., adjectives and adverbs) that describe what to express for each song as well as ways to sing those descriptors. Descriptors can be used to focus on specific musical elements that need work such as articulation, dynamics, color, and mood.

- Dedicate a poster or a section of a whiteboard in the choral room for each song the choir is preparing. Clearly list the descriptors that the students contributed.

- Lists of descriptors can be ongoing throughout the academic year.

- Laminate key descriptor words. Use a magnetic board to move descriptors to different songs as needed.

CHAPTER 16

Flashlights

*L*ooking for an innovative way to encourage the use of a full dynamic range? The flashlight gadget may provide some solutions:

- Use the flashlight to demonstrate crescendos and decrescendos on a wall in a darkened room. Show the singers the sound they created versus the desired sound.

- Line your singers up to face a wall in your choir room. Hand out flashlights to each singer in your choir. Tell them to use the flashlights to create phrases or dynamics on the wall in front of them.

- Improve contour phrasing and word emphasis by using a flashlight.

Tip:

Try a "dark" rehearsal. Not only will dynamics, phrasing, and musicianship improve, but removing the element of light heightens the sense of hearing. It will certainly be a different experience for your choir!

CHAPTER 17

Dryer Hose

*B*uying dryer hose in bulk at your local hardware or home improvement store will surely raise questions to its use. But you can confidently make the purchase knowing the dryer hose in the choral classroom will offer fresh options to teach vocal technique!

Use the plastic dryer hose for its flexible properties. Cut individual gadgets into 18" segments (or at least long enough to stretch from a student's ear to the mouth). Carefully bind the wire ends with tape for safety-sake.

- "Not me…" So many young singers do not think they are the culprit of an immature vowel or wrong note. But the dryer hose does not lie! Demonstrate how the singers should hold the dryer hose ends to the mouth and to one ear (this leaves the other ear unobstructed and open to hear the teacher model examples or to simply hear the rest of the choir).

- For singers who are experiencing pitch-matching problems, you can sing the correct pitch into the dryer hose that is held up to the student's ear. Place another student who has excellent pitch next to this singer so they are hearing accurate pitches from both sides.

- Use the dryer hose gadget to encourage blending and listening. Connect the mouth of one singer to the ear of another. Listening to each other in this way encourages teamwork and blending opportunities, as well as strengthens the individual's responsibility to singing as part of the ensemble.

- Form a singing circle and use the dryer hoses as gadgets as the choir sings their repertoire.

Tip:

The dryer hose gadget is also an excellent tool to practice dynamics, as well as breath inhalation and exhalation.

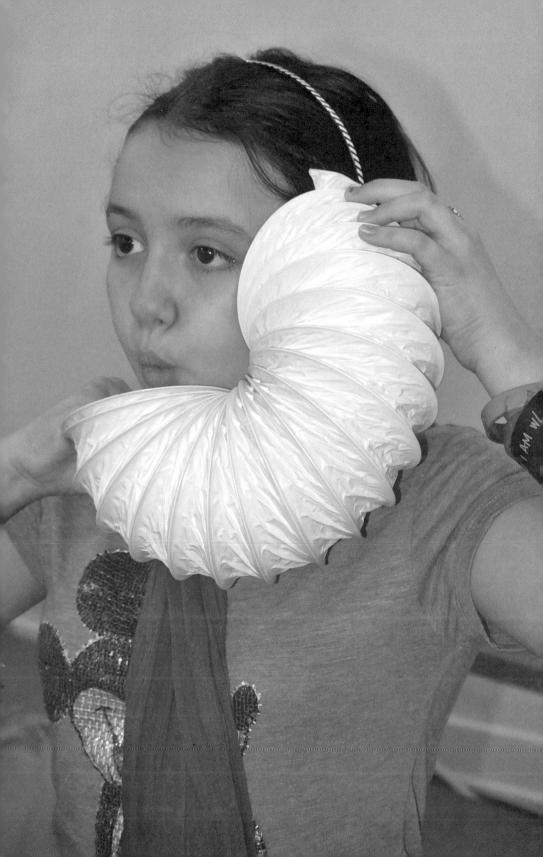

CHAPTER 18

Tools and the Toolbelt

$\mathcal{D}$uring my first year of teaching middle school, my husband's tools began to mysteriously disappear! I confessed to using the tools – quite effectively, I might add – during choir rehearsals. As a result, I received a tool belt from my father-in-law that Christmas!

Use authentic tools to add a "real life element" to solving problems with vocal and choral issues; the singers love it!

Stuff your tool belt with all sorts of things (i.e., cotton balls to real tools) to demonstrate vocal technique. Here are some of my favorites:

Pliers
Demonstrate open jaw, space in the face, relaxed hinge

Hammer and Nails of different sizes
Tapping action for staccato, accents, marcato

Scissors
Visually snip cut-offs

Paintbrush
Paint phrase contouring, articulation, dynamics, word stress, diction, and even vowel formation (see gadget #9)

Tape Measure
Measure the dynamic levels, sound of maturity, and breath.

Tip:

Add crazy things to the tool belt on a weekly basis to avoid repetition and stagnation. Be inventive as you consider items that can be used as a gadget to improve vocal technique and choral pedagogy (cotton balls, caulking gun, dart, scrub brush, cotton swabs, and children's putty, etc.)

CHAPTER 19

Clothespins

Clothespins can be a great gadget resource in your choral classroom. Need a quick posture fix? Notice singers craning their necks or rounding their shoulders? Clothespins are inexpensive and can fix problems!

- Partner up your singers. Ask one singer to stand with perfect posture. Clip a clothespin between the shoulder blades when they are in the correct position. If the singer rounds his/her shoulders or slumps in posture, the clothespin pops off.

- Use a clothespin for singers who crane forward toward the director; they can benefit by pinning a clothespin further up on the base of the neck.

- Clip clothespins to the singers' sides as an arm placement reminder.

CHAPTER 20

Twinkle Lights

A rehearsal space should be inviting and invigorating! The environment where the singers rehearse is just as important as the teaching that occurs there! Strands of twinkle lights (commonly used for Christmas decorating) can be a favorite classroom gadget to engage curiosity and create interest.

Create a "word of the week" and outline the board with colored lights.

Use twinkle lights to alert students to changes in concert information or due dates. When there is an important update or critical information has changed, turn on the blinking lights.

Use blinking lights to set the "focus" for the rehearsal. Not a second of class time is wasted by giving verbal instructions when the students can immediately see the information upon entering the room. Write instructions specific for the rehearsal, such as: no folders, concert mixed stance, or instructions to complete a rehearsal self-evaluation sheet before leaving.

Tip:

Singers are more productive if you exhibit an interest in their lives outside of choir! Create a wall space or board with lights "spotlighting" musicians in your program including their community performances as well as their accomplishment in and out of school.

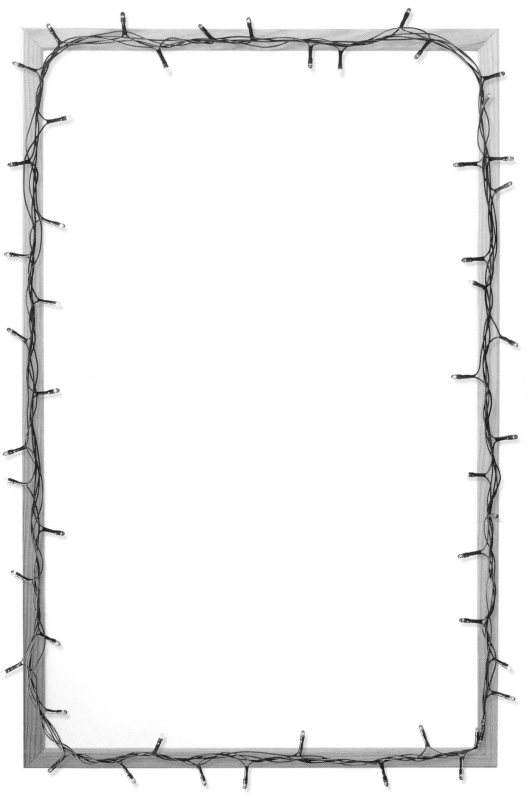

CHAPTER 21

Ladder

*T*eaching the concept of the scales and relationship between intervals can be difficult, especially if a singer does not have a background in piano. The ladder offers some visual cues in teaching these musical concepts.

- Tape both scale tones and Solfège letters on a ladder in the classroom.

- Use the ladder to demonstrate intervals. Students move hands or feet on the ladder for each interval while singing to experience moving spatially.

- Construct a ladder (or multiple ladders) on the floor to teach and work on scale and/or interval relationships.

- Turn the ladder into a staff, using the rungs as line notes.

Tip:

The ladder can also be used to demonstrate dynamic levels. Seeing the difference between rung 1 and rung 5, or physically moving one's feet from rung 1 to rung 5, can create the kinesthetic awareness needed to connect the left and the right sides of the brain.

CHAPTER 22

Ribbons, String Elastic and Belts

*B*reath is the fuel for singing. Without a thorough display of anatomy and physiology of the breathing mechanism, teaching breath inhalation, exhalation, and control can be a difficult task. The sensation of a successful breath must engage the lower abs, obliques, and even the back muscles. Try using ribbons, string, elastic and belts to teach the multi-dimensional sensation of breath.

- Tie a ribbon, string, piece of elastic, or a belt around the abdominal muscles. Center it below the belly button.

- Use any intake exercise. When filling "out with air" during the inhalation process, the belt or string will be tight around the abdominal area and the back. As the singer releases the air or sings, the belt or string will become loose.

- Move the string, ribbon, elastic, or belt up or down to feel other sensations that are not as productive.

Tips:

Hold an "ugly" belt competition. Parents clean out closets and you benefit by collecting an impressive variety of belts donated for use in the classroom.

When speaking about breath, try saying "fill out with air" instead of "fill up with air."

CHAPTER 23

Candles

A candle is a superb gadget for teaching breath concepts. Once singers fill the breath space, they often struggle with controlling that breath during the singing process.

- Using an unlit candle, the students inhale and puff gently on the wick 10 times and then until breath is exhausted. Repeat exercise increasing to 15 puffs, to 20 puffs, etc. Use the same mechanics when working on melismas or intricate passages within music. This exercise is efficient when applied to singing Renaissance or Baroque music.

- Using a lit candle, instruct responsible singers to inhale and blow a gentle, consistent stream of air that bends the flame, but not actually blowing the flame out.

- Reinforce the body's natural reaction to blowing out a candle as the breathing mechanism for blowing out a candle is the same as for singing.

- Use different sizes of candles to represent the amount of air needed for inhalation as well as how fast the air must travel out of the body.

Tip:

Bulk packages of birthday candles are great gadgets to keep in the choir classroom and can be found at party stores.

CHAPTER 24

Pantyhose

One of my favorite gadgets is a leg of (clean) pantyhose or nylons. With a multitude of options, a stocking of hose can provide ways to help with phrasing, dynamics, breath, range extension, and energy in sound.

- Tie pantyhose around a person's waist. The pantyhose now serves as a breath inhalation and exhalation gadget. When singers inhale, they should feel the expanse of their abdominal and back muscles. As they sing, the singers stretch and pull the panty hose out and away from the lower abs. This exercise encourages movement and energy in the use of air.

- Singers pull and release the pantyhose to reinforce correct placement of each breath and the contour of the phrase.

- For passages with upper register use, music with leaps, or sections that require a more engaged breath, stand on one end of the hose and pull the pantyhose up and over. The motion engages the abs and creates life in the soft palate. Also, the give and take of the hose will allow singers to feel kinesthetic resistance; they will incorporate that feeling into their musicianship.

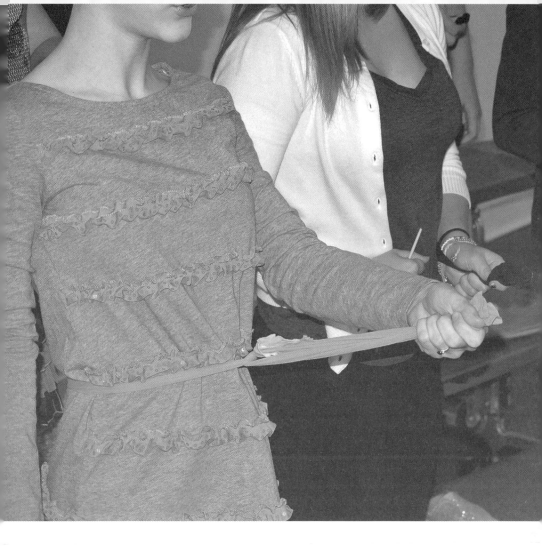

Tip:

Panty Hose Tag is a great group game. It is a good idea for your singers to keep panty hose in their folder at all times. When the mood strikes, tell singers to put the leg end of the pantyhose on their heads (not over their face). On the word, "Go!" singers attempt to pull the pantyhose off other singers' heads. The singer who grabs the most hose wins. A great prize can be a bag of candy inside hose, or if the winner is a girl, a brand new pair of pantyhose!

CHAPTER 25

Face Paint

*F*ace paint or face markers are invaluable gadgets when working on facial expression and tone development. They can be purchased at any craft store and are cheap and effective. While most face paints or face markers wipe away easily, many students like to leave the paint on as it attracts attention and makes them unique!

- Using face markers/paint, draw an upward arrow above each eyebrow. This reminds singers to lift the eyebrows on breath intake as well as singing and performing with engaged facial expressions.

- Paint dots on the face where you want singers to focus on resonation or creating a bright sound.

- Draw little arrows right above a singer's top lip to encourage a "lifted snarl," keeping the sound forward.

Tip:

My experience is that the brown markers seem to stick to skin longer than other colors. Just a word of caution: check yourself before leaving school and take a peek at yourself in the car mirror. I have been known to shop at the grocery store wearing face paint!

CHAPTER 26

Bubbles and Feathers

*I*nstilling the concept of lightness in tone or lift in tone can be difficult for singers to understand and to apply in their vocal technique. A bag of feathers or bottles of tiny bubbles can be very effective gadgets.

- Conduct with a feather or give each singer a feather.
  - Use feathers to show phrasing while singing.
  - Use feathers to bounce in staccato passages; this will encourage a light approach.
  - Circle feathers in a moving forward motion for a lift in higher notes or passages or to engage the soft palate.
- Conversely, give singers heavy weighted objects and do the same tasks. Let them experience the differences and ask them to verbally share their observations between the light and heavy objects.
- Use liquid bubbles for work on the onset of a gentle breath.

Tip:

Craft stores can be the music teacher's or choral director's ideal place to shop for gadgets and supplies! In addition to huge bags of feathers or tiny bottles of bubbles sold in bulk in the wedding section, a craft store offers lots of gadget options to incorporate into your teaching methods!

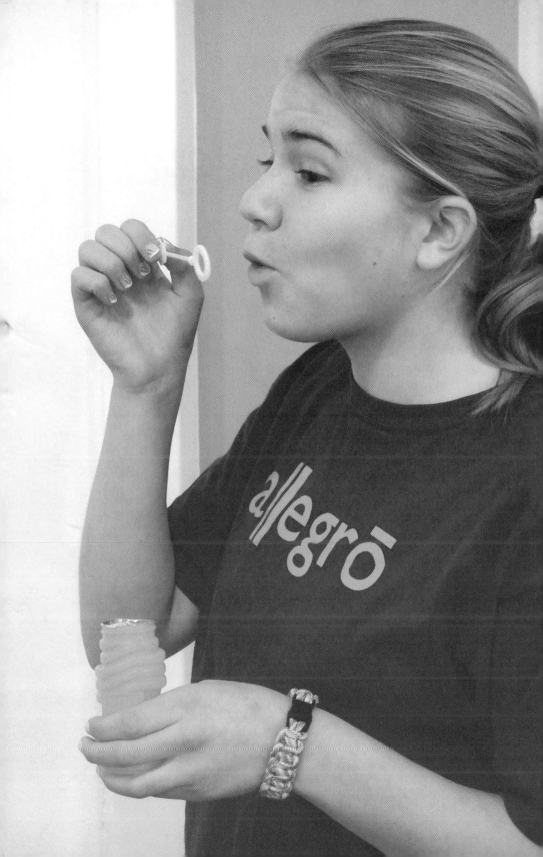

CHAPTER 27

Kids' Toys

*B*ring out the inner child in you and your singers and make a connection from the past to the present by using favorite old toys.

Magnetic Drawing Boards

Magnetic drawing boards are a good substitute when you are in a location without a chalk or white board. Use the drawing board to show phrasing and articulation. Ask around; many families have stored these types of toys in plastic storage containers. Similarly, dry erase boards are a great tool to have in your classroom, too!

Modeling Clay

Children's modeling clay can be used to sculpt vowels, dynamics, phrasing, or articulation patterns in music. This gadget is also very effective to demonstrate vowel and mouth formation. Singers can be quite adept at creating on-the-spot sculptures as a team building activity.

The Hoberman Sphere

The Hoberman sphere, a favorite of many voice teachers, is a great teaching gadget to reinforce breath, dynamics, and phrasing. The Hoberman sphere resembles a geodesic dome, but is capable of folding down to a fraction of its normal size. Colorful plastic versions can be found in the toy section in your local stores.

Vampire Teeth

Vampire teeth are an effective gadget when pulled out of a costume box or junk drawer! Vampire teeth can be used as a model for singing with lift in the cheek and upper lip while not dropping the jaw. The teeth are also a fun gadget while working on diction.

Tip:

Make a point to shop toy sections and costume departments after holidays. In the fall, the vampire teeth can easily be found in bulk and many toys that can be used as gadgets may be on clearance after the holidays.

CHAPTER 28

Sports Balls

*A*thletic equipment can be important choral gadgetry! Be inventive with how you use gadgets as many athletes are potential singers and members of your choir!

Footballs

- A perfect spiral football pass demonstrates the use of breath and the spin energy needed when singing correctly.

- The perfect football throw has a natural arch similar to a musical phrase.

- When singing a challenging leap or phrase in the music, ask the choir to simulate throwing a football. The action of throwing helps the body to engage the breath and energy for the singer.

Ping Pong Balls, Bouncy Balls, Tennis Balls

- Energy can be increased (lightness or bounce) in the sound with the use of balls.

- Singers improve when using balls to demonstrate strong and weak beats.

Beach Balls

- Filling a beach ball with air requires absolute use of the breathing mechanism.

- A beach ball, tucked in an embrace with legs in squat position, creates lift and bounce in the sound while grounding the breath.

Frisbee

- OK...a Frisbee is not a sports ball, but it is definitely fun to use! A Frisbee is a super gadget to "throw" as an upper-range developer, as well as a gentle releaser at the end of a phrase.

CHAPTER 29

Mirrors

Mirrors can be used as the perfect gadget for teaching and reinforcing the visual aspects of vowel/tone formation, facial expression, posture, and breath. Require singers to keep a handheld mirror or compact mirror in their choral folders. Install several full-length mirrors in the choral room.

Use mirrors in the following ways:

- Singers can check lip formations when singing vowels. Not only can they see how their mouths are shaped when singing the "ah" vowel, they will actually see and feel the breath against the mirror.

- Vocalists can use a mirror to check their tongue placement in the mouth. Many singers have no idea their tongue arches when singing certain vowels or consonants.

- Singers can use the mirror to watch themselves when singing and evaluate what they see. Am I animated? Are my eyes expressive? Am I engaging?

- Full-length mirrors are excellent gadgets to reinforce correct posture, motion, feet and hand placement, as well as to access their facial expressions. A full-body view provides a memorable visual to see the breath intake.

Tips:

My choir, Allegro, recently lined an entire wall with mirrors. It is incredible to rehearse with singers who are aware of their bodies.

Check with gym supply companies about acquiring full-length mirrors at a discount.

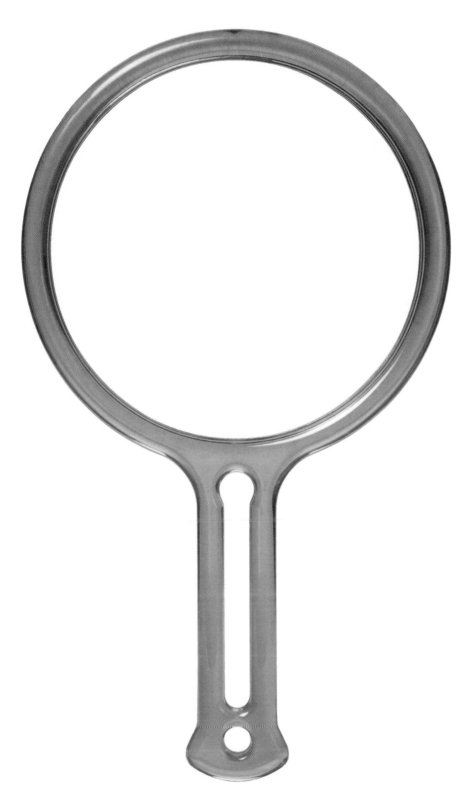

CHAPTER 30

Hands and Arms

Arms and hands are essential gadgets that are readily available, cost nothing, and offer endless possibilities! Here are a few ways to use the limbs in teaching choral music.

Consonants

Choral directors often focus so intensely on vowel uniformity that consonants are forgotten. However, consonants sung with clarity and energy "set" the vowel.

- **T:** Tap together two index fingers in shape of a T

- **G** and **K:** Karate chop with a hand

- **R:** Flip the index and middle finger to flip the **R** consonant

- **W** and **H:** Place the palm of hand in front of mouth and feel the air that hits the hand before singing the **W** and while singing the **H** consonant.

- **F** and **V:** Using two top front teeth, gently bite the bottom lip while taking an index finger from mouth outward.

- **L:** Using left hand, click the **L** consonant on like pulling a light switch (between the thumb and index finger)

Cut-offs

- **S:** Imagine that the palm of a hand is a sizzling skillet. Using the index finger from the opposite hand, tap the **S** consonant on the sizzling skillet for an introductory consonant or an ending consonant.

- **"Ih" release:** Encourage singer to end words with an "ih" release instead of an "uh" release (as the "ih" will keep the release of the pitch up instead of ending with the pitch down). Ask singers to close their index finger and thumb when singing the cut-off, release the fingers open with a lift.

     For example: Mine = Mah-nih (not Mah-nuh)

Spin

- If you are looking for ways to encourage an energetic, moving tone, try spinning or twirling the index fingers through long or held notes.

- The spin will also work with rolling arms in a circular motion in front of the body.

Articulation

- Running fingers can increase agility or clarity in moving passages. Hold one hand out with palm down, using the other hand's index and middle fingers, "run" the rhythm of the passage on your hand. Encourage singers to imitate the feel of separation in the voice.

- Use hands to karate chop (in the air or on the thighs) a rhythm pattern or any areas that need clarity. Combine karate chops with "spreading paint" (see below) for legato sections that need attention.

- Spread the paint or smooth the frosting. Use the entire body, especially the arms, when seeking long, lovely legato lines. By "spreading paint" up and down (see "#9 Paintbrushes and Paint") to create the lines to sing. Smooth the frosting using long arm arches.

- If you want to involve the entire body, the motion used in cross-country skiing is effective for a push and pull through long phrases.

ABOUT THE AUTHOR

Christy Elsner, a native Kansan, is the founder and Artistic Director of the Allegro Choirs of Kansas City. Under her direction, the Allegro choirs have grown from one choir of 38 singers to 5 choirs with over 250 singers since the year 2000. Allegro has travelled extensively nationally and internationally with performances at the White House for President and First Lady Obama, St. Peter's Basilica, Carnegie Hall, and Meyerson Hall. The choirs are frequent guests of the Kansas City Symphony.

As an active clinician for children's, youth, and treble choirs, Christy enjoys giving workshops on innovative rehearsing and unusual teaching tools. She was honored to conduct the 2012 NWACDA Children's Honor Choir and the 2012 Wyoming and Missouri All-State Children's Honor Choirs. In 2011, she shared her choral passion with honor choirs in Arkansas, Kansas, Missouri, Mississippi, and Louisiana. She was named the 2010 Kindest-Kansas Citian and the 2008 MENC Outstanding Middle Level Educator and recently completed six years as the SWACDA Children's and Community Youth R&S Chair. She is a past receipient of the KCDA Outstanding Young Conductor Award.

Christy received her music education degree from the University of Kansas and received the Marcus E. Hahn Award for Outstanding Senior in Music Education. Her professional memberships include MENC, Chorister's Guild, Chorus America, and ACDA. Christy and her husband, Sean, stay busy with their three children: Chandler, Chase, and Carlee.

NOTES

NOTES

NOTES

NOTES

NOTES